LIVING

ELIZABETH TINIUS

CHRISTIAN

A STUDY FOR TEEN GIRLS

21ST CENTURY CHRISTIAN PUBLISHING

ISBN: 978-0-89098-698-1

©2015 by 21st Century Christian

2809 12th Ave S, Nashville, TN 37204

All rights reserved.

Cover design by Jonathan Edelhuber

TABLE OF CONTENTS

LIVING Christian Series
A Study for Teenage Girls
By Elizabeth Tinius

Instead of talking about "Christian Living," our study will focus on being a Living Christian. This phrase is not necessarily used in the Bible as much as the text discusses our being live (as in "alive") in our faith: doing and not just reading or knowing. Our studies over the next weeks will focus on not just living a Christian lifestyle but living the Christian lifestyle as a living Christian.

At the beginning of this study and again at the end, I want you to consider why living Christian is so important.

Through our studies, we will be covering topics that are real and relevant to your life as a teenage girl in today's society. As a teenage girl, you have significantly different expectations and responsibilities placed on you than a teenage girl did even just ten years ago! Whatever those differences may be, we will discuss how to rise above and persevere as a Living Christian.

What is your opinion of the difference between Christian living and being a living Christian?

_____

_____

Why do you think being a Living Christian is so important?

_____

_____

_____

_____

_____

_____

OUR EXAMPLE

In the Bible we have several examples of what being a Christian is all about. The four Gospels tell us a great deal about the life of Jesus: who He was and what He did during His lifetime. His story is followed by the letters of Paul, Peter, James, John, and Jude. The history of Jesus and His biography give us the best example of what being a Living Christian is. Hebrews 4:15 states: "For we do not have a high priest who is unable to empathize with our weaknesses, but we have one who has been tempted in every way, just as we are—yet he did not sin." Jesus was divine, but He was also human in every way—He was *just* like us, yet He still set the perfect example of how to be a Living Christian.

Read Luke 4:1-13

Who tempts Jesus while He is in the desert?

What was Jesus doing?

Spiritually speaking, what does "Man does not live on bread alone" mean?

Read Luke 4:38-44

What was one of Jesus' main deeds during His ministry?

How many people did He heal and help?

Why does Jesus say He was sent?

Read Matthew 9:9-13

Jesus said, "It is not the healthy who need a doctor, but the

_____."

Jesus said, "I have not come to call the righteous, but

_____."

Who are the "sick"?

Luke 19:10 says, "For the Son of Man came to seek and to save the lost."

Jesus had one goal during His lifetime:

To _____and _____the

_____.

Our lives should follow His example. Being a Christian is not just a label; it's not just about going to church or knowing the Bible. Being a Christian is about being alive in Christ. Being alive is an *action*. You cannot be alive without doing. We should not just *be*; we must *do*.

What is the example that Jesus has set for us?

He _____for His _____.

He went out and _____.

Jesus said He was sent with the purpose to "proclaim the good news of the kingdom of God" (Luke 4:43). If Jesus is *the* example of how we should live, what does His example here imply about our purpose?

One of my favorite sayings is: "Knowledge is power." You have the power to heal and help others. What is this power?

How does this knowledge help you to be a Living Christian?

Setting Goals

Growing into a Living Christian will not happen overnight unless you are like Paul and go from one extreme of zealot to another, or you have an epiphany and feel the Spirit moving in you! Either way, you need to set goals on how to become a Living Christian.

Jesus spent time fasting in the desert and time alone in prayer. What do you need to do to prepare yourself for your ministry?

Set some goals for fulfilling your meaning and purpose.

Goal 1 _____

_____

Goal 2 _____

_____

Goal 3 _____

_____

Jesus set the ultimate goal of ministry, purpose, and life meaning as a Living Christian. He said plainly several times during His ministry that He had *the purpose to teach*, to seek out those who are spiritually sick and to help them find salvation and peace through Him. As Christians—followers of Christ—our purpose and meaning for living are exactly the same. We are on the earth for one purpose: to teach others the Good News, the gospel of Christ. Luke put it this way in Acts 20:24: "However, I consider my life worth nothing to me; my only aim is to finish the race and complete the task the Lord Jesus has given me—the task of testifying to the good news of God's grace." Similarly, Paul wrote in 1 Corinthians 2:2: "For I resolved to know nothing while I was with you except Jesus Christ and him crucified."

The knowledge of Jesus and salvation is life-changing to those who don't have knowledge of either. This knowledge is extremely powerful. You have in your possession the key to spiritual salvation.

Nothing is more important.

When you get to heaven, God will not ask if you made an "A" in algebra or if you won the district game. He won't ask you about your new car or your job. He will most likely ask, "What did you do for Me? What did you do in your lifetime to further My kingdom? How many people did you tell? Who did you help come to know Me? Did you live out the purpose I set out for you?" This is the most important activity of your life. Above everything else, God should be number one in your life and number one on your "to-do" list. Nothing else matters to God except this purpose. Now this does not mean that you should disregard your other responsibilities or that you shouldn't do anything else in life. God created us so that we can live and enjoy life. He gave us other people to be family, friends, and companions, to share our lives together and enjoy one another. He gave us amazing physical abilities that we can use for playing sports and being physically active. God wants you to live life abundantly and to be fulfilled and happy in Him. But above all, His purpose and meaning for your life should supersede everything else.

Look at the passion modeled by Paul in 1 Corinthians 2:2: "I resolved to know nothing while I was with you except Jesus Christ and him crucified." Does that mean he knew nothing else? No! But he knew that the most important thing to know was Christ and only Christ: the gospel. He knew that this is what everyone needed to know. He knew that this was the only way to bring these people to salvation. This was the only way he had any shot of changing these people's lives. Scripture states multiple times how brief our life is compared to eternity. Job says in Job 7:7, "My life is but a breath." Psalm 39:5 states, "Everyone is but a breath." Ecclesiastes 6:12 teaches, "For who knows what is good for a person in life, during the few and meaningless days they pass through like a shadow?" Take a breath. Look at a shadow. See how quickly they come and go. This is your life. You do not know when it will end; you get one shot. Make the most of it. Do what God keeps calling you to do and fulfill your purpose. Make it your goal to be a Living Christian.

CONTEMPORARY TEMPTATION

Hebrews 4:15 states, "For we do not have a high priest who is unable to empathize with our weaknesses, but we have one who has been tempted in every way, just as we are—yet he did not sin." Jesus was tempted in every way. Just like you. He knows the pressures and temptations you encounter; He experienced every one of them. Remember that at one point in His life Jesus was a teenager. When He was a teenager, He was "tempted in every way—just as we are," just like you! However He did not succumb to those temptations. He set the perfect example for us of how to overcome. Through a strong foundation of faith and trust in Him, we can overcome anything! Philippians 4:13 states, "I can do all things through him who gives me strength." All things! Through the Holy Spirit, Christ empowers us with the strength, willpower, and self-control to overcome any temptation. Think about self-control for a moment. Self-control is the *act of controlling your actions, to deny yourself, and to control your impulses*. Webster's dictionary defines self-control as: 1) the act of denying yourself, controlling your impulses; 2) control of one's behavior. You control what you say and do in every moment of your life. Thinking about your purpose and meaning, temptations seem pointless when your complete focus is fulfilling the purpose set for you by God Himself.

PERSPECTIVE: Is it easy to be tempted when your complete focus and goal is to teach others about the gospel of Jesus?

Absolutely not! If your mindset is to teach others and bring others to salvation, you will not easily fall into temptation. This is not to say that you will never fall into temptation. We are human, not divine in any way. Romans 3:23 states, "for all have sinned and fall short of the glory of God." Especially when you are a teenager, it is sometimes easy to get caught up in the moment. It seems easy to succumb to temptations when hanging out with friends who are not Christians, while in school or on trips with the band or athletics. Whenever there is a large group of peers doing an activity or participating in something that is sinful, it is sometimes easier to fall into that temptation and participate since "everyone's doing it." However, the pressure to participate is less powerful when you are among true Christian friends and people who are doing the right thing with the right focus.

Temptations will come and it's during those times of temptation that you must stand firm and be strong.

Read Proverbs 25:28

During this period of time, walls of a city were vital to the protection and survival of each city and kingdom. What does this verse mean spiritually?

Read Galatians 5:16-26

We are called to live by the _____ .

What is contrary to the Spirit?

What are some of the acts of sinful nature?

People who live in and by the sinful nature will not inherit the

_____ .

The fruit of the Spirit is: Love, _____ , Peace, Patience,

_____ , Goodness, _____ , Gentleness,

and _____ - _____ .

When we live by the Spirit we are in _____ with the Spirit.

Read 1 Thessalonians 5:4-11

This scripture states we are the "children of _____ and the children

of _____ ."

Who does Scripture say is The Light?

We need to always be alert and _____ .

Read 2 Timothy 3:1-5

Does this sound like anyone you know? What is one of the qualities of

these people? They will not have _____ - _____ .

Can you love any of these things and have self-control?

Read Titus 2:11-14

When we are baptized, what brings us salvation?

What does it teach us and help to do?

Jesus redeemed us to do and be what?

Read 1 Peter 1:13-14

13: "Set your hope on the _____ ."

"Be _____ ."

14: "As _____ children."

First Peter 5:8 admonishes, "Be alert and of a sober mind. Your enemy the devil prowls around like a roaring lion looking for someone to devour."

Read 2 Peter 1:3-8

What may we do through the precious promises given us?

What do we add to knowledge?

If we possess these qualities, what will we be able to be?

Setting Goals

Self-control is not always easy. It must be practiced and put into effect. With intent and purpose, self-control will become natural.

Set goals for strengthening your self-control. What are some ways you can strengthen your self-control and willpower? What are some areas where you need more self-control?

Goal 1 _____

_____

Goal 2 _____

_____

Goal 3 _____

_____

The underlying theme throughout these scriptures is self-control—one of the top qualities we must practice and possess to overcome temptation and live a God-centered life. To be a Living Christian you must have self-control at all times. You cannot believe, set a good example for others and yet live a sinful life. Romans 6:1 says, "Shall we go on sinning so that grace may increase? By no means!" In other words, if you plan to continue in sin knowing what you are doing, you prove that you have no understanding of God's grace. You cannot consciously continue to live in sin and expect grace, i.e., salvation. When we are baptized and give our lives to Christ, we die to sin. It should have no power over us.

God and Jesus give us all of the tools we need through the Spirit to live upright lives, even in this day when sin is rampant and it seems so easy to fall into that temptation. Consider some of the temptations you face as a teenager: to lie, drink alcohol, be disrespectful to parents, disobey parents, smoke, cheat on homework, do drugs, and give in to sexual temptations. These are real. However young or old you may be, these temptations are sometimes hard to overcome. Be on your guard and with a firm foundation, you can overcome any temptation—no matter how strong or weak you feel in the moment.

Fix on your heart the purpose God has given you; put things in perspective for your future; change your mindset with this one purpose: Over everything else, you are here to teach others. You are here to tell others and bring as many as you can to Christ. As a teenager, when you stand firm and strong in your beliefs, you make a tremendous impact on your friends and peers. They may not realize it at the time, but you are setting an example for them to see that you are different. You have this purpose for living, your purpose for being. When you follow this purpose and work toward this goal, the devil will find ways to attack you whether through friends or peers at school or when you're just hanging out. It always seems that he will attack those who work most diligently furthering the kingdom of God. *But* if you live with purpose and with self-control, this will also be the easiest time to resist temptation. With a focused heart, a focused mind, self-control, and intent and purpose as a Living Christian, you will be able to rise above any temptation that may come your way.

ABSTINENCE

A s a teenage girl in today's society, you have tremendous sexual pressures put on you. TV shows, abundance of immodest clothing, movies, music, and other media portray girls as sex objects who are expected to be sexually available. It is amazing how much it has changed in just a matter of years. Even a decade ago, I recall a lot of girls who were promiscuous, but not nearly as many as today. Today, one in four teenage girls has a sexually transmitted disease, otherwise known as an STD. That's 25 percent, or 3.2 million teenage girls. That number is even higher among the African-American population. It's close to 50 percent. Sexually transmitted diseases are not just annoying; they are harmful to your health. They can be painful, cause cervical cancer, genital warts, infertility, and can even be fatal. STDs also make a person more vulnerable to HIV, which, in most cases, leads to AIDS. In 2015, almost one million teenage girls will get pregnant. No matter what is taught about condoms, contraceptives, or any other "safe sex" education, there is no such thing as safe sex. When done outside of marriage, sex is never physically or emotionally safe (especially for girls).

God had great intentions for sex when He created the act. Sex is meant to be between one man and one woman who are married. Sex is wonderful when it's reserved for marriage. It is no wonder that once people start having sex outside of marriage there are so many undesirable consequences. Not only is the cost high from a monetary perspective, the cost is also high physically and emotionally. Most importantly, there are the high consequences spiritually and in terms of one's salvation

(1 Corinthians 6:9-10; Revelation 22:15).

Jesus, Paul, and other writers in the Bible discuss several different types of sexual sin. *Adultery* is sexual intercourse with someone other than one's spouse. *Fornication/sexual immorality* is a broader term for unauthorized sexual relations that includes adultery as well as all other sexual sins. *Prostitution or harlotry* is the selling of sexual "service." *Orgies* are sexual activities among more than two people. *Sodomy* is anal or homosexual sex between men. *Unnatural relations* is homosexual sex (gay or lesbian).

Plain and simply: You cannot be a Living Christian if you are involved in sexual sin.

Read Genesis 2:20-25

For whom was woman made?

Why?

What did God institute when He created woman?

Read Matthew 15:16-20

What are "unclean" thoughts or acts that come from the heart?

We know that all sin is equal in the eyes of God. In this scripture, Jesus compares what two sexual sins to murder?

Read 2 Corinthians 20:20-21

Paul was afraid that he would find sinners who had not repented of which sins they had been doing?

What is repentance?

If someone is involved in a sexual sin, can they be forgiven? Under what circumstances?

Read Galatians 5:19

Will anyone who practices adultery, fornication, or other sexual sin inherit the kingdom of God?

Read Hebrews 13:4

How should marriage be treated?

Read 1 Corinthians 7:1-3

Why do you think Paul writes, "It is good for a man not to marry"?

Does this mean men should not marry?

According to this scripture, what is an essential part of being married?

Setting Goals

The word *abstinence* is not in the Bible. However, the writers of the Bible put it in more simple terms: Do not commit sexual adultery or immorality. In other words, abstain from these acts. Paul puts it simply in Colossians 3:4-6: "When Christ, who is your life, appears, then you also will appear with him in glory.

Put to death, therefore, whatever belongs to your earthly nature: sexual immorality, impurity, lust, evil desires and greed, which are idolatry. Because of these, the wrath of God is coming."

Setting goals for yourself in terms of your future plans for your sexual behavior are crucial to your ability to stay pure until marriage. When you have a firm stance on your goal to stay pure before marriage, you have a much higher self will and the power to overcome any sexual temptation that will come—and it will come.

Set goals for yourself in terms of sexual intimacy. How will you stay pure? How will you abstain until marriage?

Goal 1 _____

_____

Goal 2 _____

_____

Goal 3 _____

_____

Sexual purity is one of the most important objectives a girl can have in her lifetime. Sexual immorality is also a sin against yourself. This is a "sin-on-me" sin that can cause grave consequences.

Though it's a sensitive subject, you must understand the differences between the genders when it comes to the act of sexual intercourse. For boys/men, sex is almost completely physical. Men are quite sensitive to touch. God made them this way. In many ways, men need sex. It's a physical need. On the other hand, for girls/women, sex is more emotional. As females, we are not as physically sensitive to intercourse as men. We don't need nor want sex all the time. The hormonal differences are almost polar opposites. It's easy to think of it in terms of the fuse of a firecracker. Boys/guys/men normally have extremely short fuses. All it takes is a look at a pretty girl, a touch, a kiss and they can be ready to explode at any time. Putting your hand on a guy's thigh or pressing up against him can light that fuse in an instant. Males are just so sensitive to physical touch. Now take the opposite from a female. While guys may be very quick to prepare for sex, women typically need more time for those feelings to build. Yes, we enjoy those physical feelings, but we do not typically act on those physical triggers. We act on emotions. Emotions are what will set us into overdrive. The feeling of "love" or something that we perceive is love is what we cherish most. When unmarried, girls see sex as an act of "love" while guys see it as physical pleasure. The media has had such a huge impact on society in terms of sex by often portraying girls and women as sexual objects. It is no wonder that more and more teenagers are starting to become sexually active at much younger ages.

Thinking back on my college days I dated a lot of guys. At one point I was "dating" five guys at once. (I laugh at that now.) Do you know how many of those guys would have had sex with me? All of them. I could have had sex with pretty much any guy to whom I would have given myself. That is the difference between a Living Christian and a girl of the secular world. I was not just going to settle for any guy out there. I wanted the best man for me. I saved myself for the one man God had prepared to give to me. I was not like most girls who would do anything with anyone just because they could. This set me apart; it made me different. Above all, I gained more respect from my boyfriends during that time than some girls have in their entire lifetime. When you have voluntary sex with someone who is not your husband, whether they say it or not, that person likely loses respect for you. You are no longer a person deserving of respect; you are a sexual object there at their leisure. There is an old phrase, "Why buy the cow when you can get the milk for free?" It's no wonder that so many girls who are sleeping around and have multiple partners in their lifetime end up unhappy, divorced, or as single, unmarried mother. And that doesn't count those who now have a disease they will carry with them the rest of their lives. So many girls fall into the trap of thinking "He's the one," and they end up breaking up following their first sexual experience. How many people do you think have actually stayed with and married the first person with whom they had sex? I think it is safe to say that it's a small percentage. You will not know he is "the one" until you've exchanged vows. Plainly stated, a guy who wants you to have sex with him before there is a commitment does not respect you.

The Bible states clearly that any sexual activity outside of marriage is a sin. When you have sex before you are married, you are committing adultery against the person you will someday marry. Any person who has been sexually active before she is married is stained. We know that we can be forgiven and be washed of that sin, but as with any sin, this is one that should be avoided. The guilt, the "dirty" feeling, and the knowledge that you have done wrong is a terrible burden to bear. Sex before marriage weighs on you when you know it is wrong. It can also tear you apart emotionally, especially if/when you end up breaking up with that person, becoming pregnant, or contracting a sexually transmitted disease. Once you are married, you can have sex for the rest of your life. Patience is a virtue, especially when it comes to sex.

Abstinence is the only way to keep yourself pure. At times it can be difficult, especially when you think you are in love with your boyfriend.

If you are engaged it can be especially difficult to wait, but you can do it. God gives us the strength we need to persevere through this temptation. The best feeling in the world is knowing you have waited for God's best. If you are pure and your husband is pure, sharing that most precious moment together on your wedding day is rare, precious, and as Christian women, is what we are called to be. Purity is a trait of a Living Christian.

Facts about STD's:

(1) http://www.iht.com/articles/2008/03/12/healthscience/12std.php

(2) http://www.npr.org/templates/story/story.php?storyId=88144955
    Number of Teenage Pregnancy: http://community.michiana.org/
    famconn/teenpreg.html

FRIENDS, BOYFRIENDS, AND PEER PRESSURE

In lesson 2, we discussed temptation and how we have the power to avoid all sorts of temptations when our focus is on our purpose as a Living Christian. In lesson 3, we examined the importance of abstinence and purity as traits of a Living Christian. Both of these categories of your life depend a great deal on with whom you hang out: who your friends and boyfriends are. Friends and boyfriends can be the best, yet most complicated part of our lives. When you are a teenager, you are with your friends almost every day. You go through many experiences together in school, sports, or other extracurricular activities. If you have a boyfriend at school, you go through those experiences with him as well. (You may have a boyfriend who does not go to your school, but it is probable that you communicate just as much by texting, emailing, i-chatting, or talking over the phone.) These are the people with whom you are in communication every day for up to 15 hours a day.

Since you spend such a great deal of time with your friends, they are the ones who likely have the greatest impact and influence on you and your future. Friends, also known as your *peers*, influence your decisions and way of thinking. This is one of the reasons why carefully choosing your friends and boyfriends is important. Choosing friends and boyfriends who share common interests and goals with you is essential to creating lifelong, valuable friendships. You want friends and boyfriends who will be assets to you in your objective of being a Living Christian.

Being selective about those with whom you "hang out" will determine the types of activities you do together and the experiences you will share. If you have friends who are not Christians, you may have a lot in common, but you will not be able to create deep relationships because you will not share the same goals in life since that person hasn't yet discovered his/her purpose that God intended for all of us. Conversely, if your friends are Christians, you will have the same goals, share the same purpose, and have the same frame of mind and way of thinking.

Perspective: What are some activities you do with your friends that help you in your walk with God? What are some activities that are harmful?

The Bible is a great source of how to choose friends and boyfriends. The Bible also gives us warning signs for which to be watchful and how to be careful when choosing our friends.

Proverbs 12:26 teaches, "The righteous choose their friends carefully, but the way of the wicked leads them astray." What does this mean?

Read Psalms 1:1-3

What is the "council of the wicked"?

What would you consider "council of the wicked" today?

How does this compare to peer pressure?

Read James 4:4

What does "friendship with the world" mean?

What does this imply about your friends?

Read 1 Corinthians 15:33-34

What does "Bad company corrupts good character" mean regarding teenage friends?

Read 2 Corinthians 6:11-7:1

Paul says do not be _____together with unbelievers.

What does "yoked" mean?

Why is this important?

Give an example of being yoked with an unbeliever.

What is the implication here concerning boyfriends?

Read 1 John 2:15-17

John tells us to not love the _____.

What does this mean to you?

Setting Goals

At this point in your life, you already have close friends whether they are Christian or not. However, these will not be the only friends you have in your lifetime, and it is probable that once you graduate and move away from home, you will find yourself finding and making new friends. Being selective about with whom you hang out and into whom you put your trust and confidence is important. It is important that you have a close friend or boyfriend that will help you in your goal of being a Living Christian. Set goals for yourself in terms of friendship and boyfriends to develop closer relationships with those who are going to help you be a Living Christian. How can you develop these relationships? What can you do to grow together spiritually? How can you avoid peer pressure?

Goal 1 _____

_____

Goal 2 _____

_____

Goal 3 _____

_____

Your friends and everyone else your age are your peers. If you have peers who have common goals and interests, you do not have to worry as much about peer pressure. If you have friends who do not share your goals, peer pressure is high. Temptations to do things because "everyone else is doing it" become harder to resist. Most girls want to be accepted in the eyes of their peers, friends, and boyfriends, which makes them susceptible to peer pressure. This is yet another reason why choosing your friends and peers with whom you spend your time is important. You don't want friends or boyfriends who try to pressure you into doing things you don't want to do or that you know are wrong. A true friend will never ask you to do something that is against your beliefs or your conscience. A true friend will also never ask you to do anything that is sinful or that is against the teachings of the Bible. Likewise, a boyfriend who really cares about you will always do what is in your best interests.

A Word on Boyfriends

Situations can be tricky when it comes to boyfriends. In most instances, girls tend to want to impress their boyfriends or boys they would like to see become their boyfriends. Girls sometimes only choose a boyfriend because of how he looks, if he is popular, or because of other outside qualities. Sometimes girls accept a boyfriend because he is the first or perhaps the only boy to ask them out. For relationships that are valuable, beneficial, and that will help you in your walk with God, you must be selective and look deeper into people than what they show on the surface. A really good read for dating is *I Kissed Dating Goodbye* by Joshua Harris.

If I might offer a bit of advice on dating, you should make a list of the qualities you want in a guy before you begin dating someone. Write down everything. I made a list when I was 14, which I still have to this day, of every single quality I wanted in a guy from looks, to heart, to attitude, even down to the kind of clothes I wanted him to wear. I had everything written down, and if someone in whom I was interested didn't fit every quality, then I didn't date that person. (Go to Appendix A, and write down the qualities you want in your boyfriend, realizing that these are the attributes you are looking for in someone who you want to be your lifelong husband and companion.)

One thing to remember in terms of friends and boyfriends is that any relationship that is beneficial to you in your walk with God should be centered on Him. Now it may not start out that way, and it may take a long time to get to that point, but for you to be kindred spirits, the Holy Spirit must be at the apex of that triangle. Every relationship should have God as first priority and you as second priority. When my husband proposed to me, he got down on his knees and said these exact words: "I want to do two things in my life: love God and love you. Will you marry me?" We have a wonderful marriage, and that is partially because we have both put God first in our lives. Sometimes we slip; neither of us is perfect, and we both fail each other at times, but when we remember that our first priority is to put God first, our relationship becomes even stronger. Each trial you face, each struggle, every time something goes wrong in your relationships—when you put God first, those trials, struggles, and hard times will heal themselves, and your relationship will become stronger. When you have a deep cut on your body, your skin heals itself with a stronger tissue, often in the form of a scar, so that the skin that was cut is much stronger than before. It is the same way with relationships. Every time you overcome a "cut" in the form of hurt feelings, a wrong done, betrayal, or disagreement, that part of your relationship will be stronger than ever if God is the center of that relationship. God-centered relationships with friends or a boyfriend is a trademark of a Living Christian.

HOMOSEXUALITY
AND SECULAR THOUGHTS

In the last 20+ years, our society has started to decay. The word *secular* means "of the world, contrary to spiritual or faith-based," which is from God or based on God. In the secular world, many of the morals and ethics that were once so influential in making decisions are now obsolete. Morals and ethics have taken a back seat to what people want now and the fact that many people want to live their lives how they want to live them. They don't know the difference between right and wrong. They don't want people to tell them what they are doing is wrong, especially when they don't think it's wrong. From the secular perspective, they truly believe that what is wrong is right and what is right is wrong. What is worse is that many ideas and actions that used to be unacceptable and considered immoral or unethical are now not only accepted, but also considered normal and even welcomed.

Perspective: What are some ideas or concepts your peers believe are right, but are, in fact, wrong?

One action that is wrong but is beginning to be socially accepted is homosexuality. Homosexuality is not a new idea, nor is it a new concept that those who practice homosexuality should be accepted and praised for who and what they are. Homosexuality started long ago and is first mentioned in the Bible in the book of Genesis. As defined by what they did, homosexuality is referred to as sodomy, which refers to the sexual act that the men from Sodom did and also as "unnatural relations" (Romans

1:26). Homosexuality is an abomination to God, as clearly and directly stated in the Bible. However that may be, homosexuality has somehow in recent years become considered normal and is no longer considered immoral. It's now considered an important part of our society.

The numbers of teen homosexuals has risen by hundreds over the last few years. The homosexuals who have set out their agenda have succeeded in working to convince everyone that homosexual feelings are normal and healthy. Perhaps you know of several teens—boys and girls alike—at your school who believe they are homosexual. Many high schools and colleges now have gay and lesbian clubs or programs to help the teen homosexual population. However this may seem acceptable in a secular viewpoint, it is not acceptable in the eyes of God.

Read Genesis 19:4-7; 24-25

What does God to do these cities?

What is the sexual sin the men of this city committed?

Leviticus 18:22 mandates, "Do not have sexual relations with a man as one does with a woman; that is detestable."

This is a direct _____ from God.

Leviticus 20:13 warns, "If a man has sexual relations with a man as one does with a woman, both of them have done what is detestable. They are to be put to death; their blood will be on their own heads."

Based on these two verses, which are direct commands from God, how does God feel about homosexuality?

Read Deuteronomy 23:17

God also includes _____ in his commands on the subject of homosexuality.

Read Judges 19:22-23.

What are the men of this city?

What are some adjectives the man uses to describe what they want to do?

Read Matthew 19:4-6

God made us _____ and _____ .

In your own opinion, why do you think God made us male and female? What was the purpose?

In these verses, Jesus teaches about marriage. Does this leave any room for "unions" of any other type?

Read Romans 1:20-32

What does Paul say these people did?

Paul describes what they did as shameful. What are some of the sins he mentions alongside sexual sin?

Read 1 Corinthians 6:9-10

Homosexuals will not _____the kingdom of God.
First Corinthians 6:18 instructs, "Flee from sexual immorality. All other sins a person commits are outside the body, but whoever sexually sins, sins against their own body."

Homosexual acts are perverse. With regard to sexual immorality, why is homosexual activity also sinful?

Read 1 Timothy 1:9-11

This verse states the law was made for _____ .
Why do you think Timothy writes this?

Read Jude 5-7

Jude states the people of Sodom and Gomorrah gave themselves over

to _____ and _____.

God detests homosexual behavior and states that it is an abomination to Him. He detests it so much He destroyed two large cities because they were overrun by homosexuals. We know from the Bible that homosexuality is not only wrong, it is also unnatural and not healthy. God created us male and female because we complement each other. Not only in body parts, but in our ways of thinking and our tendencies. He knew that what Adam needed was not just a friend, Adam needed a confidant. He needed someone who would complement him and give him total satisfaction physically and emotionally. He made a woman for Adam.

Homosexuals are not only gender-confused, many are unhappy and dissatisfied. Many believe they are homosexual because of sexual or mental abuse, teasing by their peers, or in need of attention from their same sex parent. Many have single parents or are being raised by grandparents.

Though homosexuality is pushed by society, the media, and special interest groups, it is a choice: a lifestyle choice. While growing up, many teens have thought themselves to be homosexual. Sometimes heterosexual teens, as well as adults, have homosexual feelings. However, having these feelings is not the same as acting on the feelings. Feelings may very well be a red flag that we are close to trouble. "I was so angry that I could have slapped him." "I just felt like tearing up my term paper right in front of her." These may be genuine feelings, and those feelings could quickly lead to big trouble if acted upon.

Someone may have homosexual feelings and choose not to act upon those feelings. The major problems (and sin) come when we give in to the lifestyle. You have to choose to live the lifestyle, and you have to choose to continue in that lifestyle. These are all choices. Consider everyone. Every single person on this earth is a liar. At one point in time, everyone has lied, whether it is a "white" lie or a great lie. As a teenager, there is no doubt that you have been tempted to lie to your parents to avoid getting in trouble or to keep secrets. At some point you have had to choose whether or not to lie. If you did, you also had to choose to continue in that lie or tell the truth. If you decided to tell the truth, the temptation will come again, but you have to continue to do what is right and continue to tell the truth. It is the same with homosexuality. People have to choose to turn to that lifestyle. They choose whether or not to continue to live in that lifestyle. The secular world says that is OK, healthy, and normal, but we know that it is not. The fact is that many people who may have thought they were gay or homosexual were helped back onto the right path and now live normal, healthy lives. Did you know there are programs available to help teens and adults who are experiencing sexuality confusion? Most people who have been helped are now ex-homosexuals and live normal, healthy, and (most often) much happier lives as heterosexuals—the way God intended.

The hard part as Christians is what to do when we come across someone who believes he or she is a homosexual. God wants us to love everyone. It's customary for Christians to adopt the philosophy to "love the sinner, not the sin" because we know that we are not perfect in any way. However, loving someone does not mean you have to accept what he or she is doing. Remember the true definition of love: doing what is in someone's best interest. Knowing exactly how to treat someone who believes he is homosexual can be difficult. Sometimes we don't know how to act or what to say. As a teenager, it can be even more challenging to know what to say or how to act because society keeps pushing the homosexual agenda and wants us to believe that it is acceptable. The simple fact is that you cannot have an impact on someone you are not willing to befriend. I once had a friend who believed himself to be gay. He lived with his "boyfriend" and was submerged in the lifestyle. We met at work and started talking. We would talk about all sorts of different subjects, and I soon learned he was gay. At first I didn't know what to say or how to react. To tell the truth, I had never known anyone who thought of themselves as gay and this kind of took me by surprise. What I did not do was react negatively or harshly, I simply said "OK." I had a choice to make: befriend or leave behind. I decided to befriend. After all, up to that point, we were getting along really well. As we spent more time together and talked more, I learned that his grandmother (who really didn't care about him) was the person who raised him. He was starving for male attention and found it in the gay community. Through our conversations, I told him, gently, that I did not agree with his lifestyle choice. I tried to get him to think outside of his box, into his future, and into what other options he had. At first he was rather standoff-ish. But after time, he started coming around. He was insecure and unhappy. I urged him to think about his future and nudged him to consider about leaving the lifestyle and going "straight." I don't know how deep an impact I had on him, but I do know that I did leave my mark. I pray now that he has changed his lifestyle. If I had reacted brashly or judgmental, he probably wouldn't have given me the time of day. He needed to know that I sincerely cared about him. I had to nurture and kindle a friendship before I could help him. That does not mean that you should befriend the first person you find, it means that if you meet someone who believes themselves to be homosexual, think first about that person, what is in their best interests, and consider how you can help them. You may already have a friend who believes himself/herself to be homosexual. In this instance, you have an open door to help someone. Remember: No one wants to be told what she is doing is wrong when she likes what she's doing. You may have a friendship in which you can boldly and directly say that the friend is doing wrong, but you will find most people can be easily hurt or offended when you confront them, and that may close any window of opportunity for you to help.

Setting Goals

Knowing exactly what to say and how to help is difficult and thought-provoking. As a Living Christian, you need to be armed with the knowledge of how to help someone. Set goals for yourself in terms of how to react and treat someone who believes himself/herself to be homosexual. What will you do or say? How can you be a good example? How you can have an influence on that person? Become acquainted with programs and counselors who can help.

Goal 1 _____

_____

Goal 2 _____

_____

Goal 3 _____

_____

From high school to college, Tom had several girlfriends. He went to church and considered himself a Christian, just a normal guy. However, at school a lot of the guys teased him. They called him "gay," among other names. Tom thought he was normal, but after a while, the teasing really got to him, and he thought he might be gay. At first, he ignored his thoughts, but the teasing continued, and Tom finally believed himself to be gay. Unsure of what to do, he went online and started meeting people. He set up a date with a guy out-of-town and went to meet him. Not really sure of what he was doing, he waited nervously until he realized he had been stood up. He called a friend, Bill, who lived in town and asked if he could stay the night at his place. When he got there, Bill, an old college buddy, inquired as to why he was in town, as it was odd that he had called so late out of the blue. Tom confided to Bill about the "date" and everything that had progressed to this point. Bill, though shocked, asked a lot of questions and then started to give Tom advice. Bill, a Christian, had never encountered this situation, but he knew that he must say something to help Tom since it was obvious Tom was on the wrong path and was confused. They talked through the night until Tom came to the realization that he knew he was wrong and needed help. When he returned home, Tom sought out a counselor and got help. A few years later, Bill learned that Tom was happily married and that he and his wife were expecting their first child. Bill could never have been used in such a way if he had automatically accused and judged.

This is a true story (with names changed).

You may never come across anyone who believes himself or herself to be homosexual, or you may be overwhelmed with friends or family who believe they are homosexuals. You never know when you may have the opportunity to help or set a good example. As Christians we must always be prepared for any situation when we will have an opportunity to share the good news. So, if/when you're given the opportunity to possibly help someone, what will you do? What will you say? How can you help someone turn back to the straight and narrow? Remember God can and will use you in ways you never imagined if you let Him. Be available, be ready, and God will use you as a Living Christian.

Ministry Resources:

Exodus Ministry: http://exodusinternational.org/

Counsel Care Connection: http://www.counselcareconnection.org/categories/Homosexual-Issues/

Living Hope Ministry: http://livehope.org/

Focus on the Family: http://www.focusonthefamily.com/topicinfo/Homosexuality_Resources.pdf

MODESTY

In today's society, modesty is largely considered irrelevant. Many of the younger generations don't even know what modesty is. Modesty has been labeled as "old-fashioned," out-of-style, and out-of-date. However, this is not what Christian women, or any woman for that matter, should think or believe. We are called to be modest, to dress modestly and be modest at all times. Simply put, modesty means covering your body. Though this may not seem important, it is not just for ourselves, but as being obedient and in service to God. Why is this so important? Why does God call us to be modest? To get the best picture, and to open our eyes completely, the only way we can even partially grasp the *why* is by viewing at the women's physique from a male point of view. Let's look at it as much as possible from a man's perspective.

As we learned in our lesson about abstinence, men are generally more strongly driven by their sex drive than women. No matter who they are, what they do, whether they are ministers, church leaders, youth leaders, or if they work a secular job, they are all made for sex. Most men need sex, plain and simple. And even more powerfully, most men want sex. This is not a bad thing, for God made them this way. God made woman for man, and He made man for woman. But men tend to have less willpower and self-control. They like to look at women, and what they see easily excites them. They are easily aroused and easily captured. And that is what we have to keep in mind, because the way we dress not only affects us, but we have an influence on everyone who sees us. Men are men, and although this is no excuse for being sinful, for those who are

Christians, having this temptation in such a great magnitude consistently is many times too much. It can easily cause them to bow to the temptation and sin of lust. We all know that every man will be called to account for his own sin. However, he is not the only one to blame, woman are to blame; as well for being the cause and source of temptation.

This is one reason why it is so important for us to dress modestly: we set an example for everyone who sees us by the way we dress ourselves. Matthew 5:28 admonishes that "anyone who looks at a woman lustfully has already committed adultery with her in his heart." This is sin. When you dress immodestly, you are inviting men to look at you. You are showing them exactly what they want to see, and many times, you are making them sin by lusting after you. Lust is not touching, holding, or anything physical. Lust takes place in someone's mind and heart when they go past just looking, and into meditating on it, thinking on it. This leads to fantasies in the mind. The sad part is, this also makes you guilty. The fact is that men would find something sexy about women despite how we choose to dress. With all of the skin that is shown today, men don't have to use their imagination anymore. They are shown exactly what they want to see. That's why Victoria's Secret is no secret at all. Breasts are exhibited everywhere for men to see, and there is no shame in being a model for underwear, bikinis, and lingerie. Nudity is everywhere. Dressing immodestly by showing cleavage, legs (referring to bottom-length shorts), and mid-drift is also referred to as being "suggestive." It is suggestive because it implies that you are *suggesting* (specifically to any guy or man who looks at you) that you are available for sex. Why else would a woman dress that way? Women who dress this way are also part of the reason why women, in general, have lost respect from men and why men have been able to degrade and exploit women so easily for their own satisfaction and even for profit.

Perspective: What are some examples of immodesty you see in everyday life?

As Christian women, we must be different. Be set apart. Dress modestly. Plain and simple. We are not our own, we are God's. We represent Christian women as a whole. Especially when we are around others who know we are Christians, we must set a good example at all times. We must do it not only to be an example, but also as a representation of our commitment to God who sees and knows everything we do. Even for those who do not know specifically that we are Christians, when we are different from everyone else, people will notice. We are vessels of God. Jesus Christ lives in us, in our hearts. We are a temple of God, and we must treat our bodies as such. We must respect our temple, because, once again, it is not our own. Your body is not yours, and mine is not mine. We belong to God.

Read 2 Timothy 2:9-10

What does Paul say about how women should dress?

Read 1 Peter 3:3-4.

Again, how does Peter say women should dress?

Does this mean that women cannot wear jewelry or nice clothes?

Although this passage is about husbands and wives, the reference of how women should dress and conduct themselves refers to all women, not just those who are married.

Read Proverbs 31:25,30

This virtuous woman clothes herself with _____

and _____.

This proverb also states that _____ is passing.

What does this statement mean? What does this have to do with modesty?

Read 1 Corinthians 3:16

According to Paul, you are the _____ of God, and the Holy

Spirit _____ inside you.

Read 1 Corinthians 6:19

You are _____ your own.

What does this verse mean? Is this physical, spiritual, or both? How does this connect with being modest?

Second Corinthians 6:16 states:

"...For we are the temple of the living God..."

The question we must then ask is how do we define "modesty" in our society? There are many definitions of modesty. In earlier times, if you showed your ankles, you were showing too much flesh. Or in other cultures, if you showed your wrist, or even your face (down to your eyes), you were showing too much. In our society, though, things are different. Standards are different. We wear shorts, short-sleeved shirts, and skirts. We like to wear cool clothing in the summer, including swimwear. So where is the line? What standard should we as Christians, being set apart, set for ourselves? Where do we draw the line? There is no specific set of rules in the Bible, or anywhere else for that matter to define modesty for our society. Many girls will not understand why we set certain parameters, so this could be an opportunity for ministry when we do set an example by dressing modestly. We have to set our own standard. Think about what is accepted in our society and how we can dress modestly in our own society. Here are some tips on how to dress modestly:

- Wear shorts that are hemmed close to the knee. Longer shorts can be cute, cool, and still stylish.

- Wear Capri pants instead of shorts. They are not only stylish, but they are also cool enough to wear in the summer. You can find them virtually everywhere, and they are long enough to cover everything.

- If you must wear spaghetti-strapped camis, wear shirts that have thicker straps and are higher cut. Exposing even some of the breast is immodest.

- Wear shirts that cover your entire core. Mid-drifts that expose hips, the belly button, and the entire waist line are immodest. Longer shirts are in style and not only go all the way down to the hips; they are extremely cute and modest.

- Wear "mini" skirts that are knee-length. Longer skirts will still keep you covered when you are sitting. Shorter skirts tend to continue to hike up when you are seated, exposes not only the legs, but often times what's beneath the skirt.

- Wear fully backed shirts and dresses. Backless tops are immodest.

- Wear full bathing suits with shorts and a sleeveless shirt or cami over it. This sometimes seems inconvenient, but it is better to be modest than not. Just because you are at a beach or swimming pool where everyone else is half-naked doesn't mean you must be half-naked too. You can still have fun and be modest!

Being modest does not mean that you are out-of-style, or that you have to wear floor-length, long sleeved dresses with a shirt hiding everything. It just means that you must cover yourself. There are a ton of clothes that are really cute, stylish, and even sexy, that are still modest. Once you learn how to put together cute, modest outfits you just might find that you are the one doing the trend setting at school, work, or church.

~A Note on Bikinis~

Should a Christian woman or girl, or any woman or girl for that matter, wear a bikini in public? From a Christian point of view and by reflecting on what we just read about modesty and how our bodies are God's temple, the answer is an emphatic *no*. You may have noticed that I stated that wearing a bikini is a source of nudity, and I whole-heartedly believe this to be true. When you think about it, all a bikini is, is a bra and underwear made of special material. All bikinis show the bottom, most of the breast, as well as every other curve a woman has. When a girl wears a bikini, she leaves little to the imagination. Just because you are at a swimming pool, beach, or water park doesn't make it OK to walk around basically naked simply because everyone else is. Men and boys are even more apt to lust in this situation, again making you both in the wrong. I can't express enough how sacred your body is. The fact that God is in you and that He views you as sacred means that it's your responsibility to take care of that precious gift. Save it for your future husband.

DEALING WITH PARENTS

There are many different dynamics of relationships between girls and their parents. Some girls are best friends with their parents and have a close, open relationship. Some girls are close to their mom but not their dad or are close with their dad but not their mom. Some girls come from single-parent homes or home situations in which the mom and dad are split but not divorced. The list of situations could go on and on. However your relationship is with your parents at this stage in life, it is still probable that *sometimes* you may have difficulties in dealing with your parents. Isn't it amazing how parents are often your best friends and then other times, they seem like they are prison guards. If you have a great relationship with your parents, this lesson will simply support you in your relationship. If you do not have a great relationship with your parents, use the information presented here to help you in dealing with your parents.

Obedience. Submission. Compliance. Because I say so. How many times have you asked "why" and the answer was, "Because I say so"? How many times have you asked to do something, and the answer was simply *no*, with no explanation whatsoever? At times, it may seem fairly difficult to get along with your parents. After all, you want freedom, yet they hold the reins. Think about any time you have had an argument with your parents, and I can tell you with great accuracy the circumstances surrounding the argument. Almost every argument with a parent is going to be based on when you leave the house. You want to go out with friends or a boyfriend, you want to take the car, you want to

49

stay out later than curfew, or you broke curfew. Am I right? Nearly every argument (that does not involve you as the daughter in "trouble") with parents is centered around these particular situations. So how can you make those situations less frustrating for you *and* your parents? How can you come to an agreement that satisfies both you and your parents?

The first thing you need to realize is that your parents love you and only want what is best for you. (I'll bet you have heard that before.) Yes, you are now a teenager who is old enough to make *some* of your own choices and decisions, but perhaps not all. You may also be responsible, mature, and trustworthy—all great attributes of a young lady. However, your parents still have the responsibility before God to raise you, care for you, and to keep you safe from all dangers—physical as well as spiritual. Think of yourself from you parents' point-of-view. You were their baby. They raised you from infancy, helped you along, and taught you. They witnessed your first step, heard your first word, and experienced all of your other "firsts." They held you when you cried and tucked you in at night. They cooked and cleaned for you, took you places, read to you, and cuddled with you. You drove them crazy at times, but through every bit of it, they loved you, and they still love you. Try to imagine the responsibility of caring for someone you love so much. That parenting role never goes away simply because you've gotten older. And the responsibility your parents carry for you now is even greater now that you are starting to make your way in the world.

Perspective: Why do you think the responsibility of your parents for you is greater now than it was when you were little?

The Bible clearly states how parents are to treat their children, as well as how children are to treat their parents. Let's start with how parents are supposed to treat their children. In reading and studying these verses, think about all of the responsibility placed on parents by God—it's tremendous.

Read Isaiah 49:15

How does this verse portray a mother's view of her child?

Read the following passages. Parents are charged with two responsibilities. Think about them as you read through these passages.

"Impress them on your children. Talk about them when you sit at home and when you walk along the road , when you lie down, and when you get up" (Deuteronomy 6:7).

"Children are a heritage from the LORD, offspring is a reward from him" (Psalms 127:3).

"My son, do not despise the Lord's discipline, and do no resent his rebuke, because the Lord disciplines those he loves, as a father whose son he delights in" (Proverbs 3:11-12).

"He who spares the rod hates their children, but the one who loves his children is careful to discipline them" (Proverbs 13:24).

"Discipline your children, for in that there is hope; do not be a willing party to their death" (Proverbs 19:18).

"Start children off on the way they should go, and even when they are old they will not turn from it" (Proverbs 22:6).

"Do not withhold discipline from a child; if you punish them with the rod, they will not die. Punish them with the rod and save them from death" (Proverbs 23:13-14).

"Listen to your father who gave you life, and do not despise your mother when she is old" (Proverbs 23:22).

"A rod and a reprimand impart wisdom, but a child left undisciplined disgraces his mother. Discipline your child and they will give you peace; they will bring you the delights you desire" (Proverbs 29:15,17).

"Fathers, do not imbitter your children, or they will become discouraged" instead, bring them up in the training and instruction of the Lord" (Ephesians 6:4).

"Fathers, do not provoke your children, lest they become discouraged" (Colossians 3:21).

"He must manage his own family well and see that his children obey him, and he must do so in a manner worthy of full respect. (If anyone does not know how to manage his own family, how can he take care of God's church?)" 1 Timothy 3:4-5.

These are just a few of the verses in the Bible about parenting. There are two main ideas here:

1. Parents should _____
   their children about God and His Word.

2. Parents should _____
   their children.

With so many verses dedicated to parenting, it is obvious that the way a parent raises his/her child is extremely important to God. When you think about it, a parent's duty is to be the first one to teach his child about God, which is the start of that child's learning about God, God's will for our lives, and salvation. Parents are commanded to raise their children in such a way that will bring glory to God. Does this change your view at all on your parent's responsibility to God and to you?

Now let's look at the verses directed at children, which means sons or daughters of any age. Think of these verses as specifically talking to you.

"Honor your father and your mother, so that you may live long in the land the LORD your God is giving you" (Exodus 20:12).

"Honor your father and your mother, as the LORD your God has commanded you, so that you may live long and that it may go well with you in the land the LORD your God is giving you" (Deuteronomy 5:16).

"Cursed is anyone who dishonors their father or mother" (Deuteronomy 27:16).

"The proverbs of Solomon: A wise son brings joy to his father, but a foolish son brings grief to his mother" (Proverbs 10:1).

"A wise son brings joy to his father, but a foolish man despises his mother" (Proverbs 15:20).

"Whoever robs their father and drives out their mother is a child who brings shame and disgrace. Stop listening to instruction, my son, and you will stray from the words of knowledge" (Proverbs 19:26-27).

"Even small children are known by their actions, so is their conduct really pure and upright?" (Proverbs 20:11).

"Listen to your father, who gave you life, and do not despise your mother when she is old. The father of a righteous child has great joy; a man who fathers a wise son rejoices in him. May your father and mother rejoice; may she who gave you birth be joyful!" (Proverbs 23:22, 24-25).

"Whoever robs their father or mother and says, 'It's not wrong, is no transgression,' is partner to one who destroys" (Proverbs 28:24).

"The eye that mocks a father, that scorns an aged mother, will be pecked out by the ravens of the valley, will be eaten by vultures" (Proverbs 30:17).

"Children, obey your parents in the Lord, for this is right. 'Honor your father and mother'—which is the first commandment with promise—'so that it may be well with you and you may enjoy long on the earth'" (Ephesians 6:1-3).

"But if a widow has children or grandchildren, these should learn first of all to put their religion into practice by caring for their own family and so repaying their parents and grandparents, for this is pleasing to God" (1 Timothy 5:4).

"Children, obey your parents in everything, for this pleases the Lord" (Colossians 3:20).

These are direct commands to you from God! Even though these verses all say "son," they refer to all children. As a daughter you have the responsibility of honoring your parents as well as obeying them.

What do you think it means to *honor* your parents?

Why do you think God has placed so much importance on your behavior as a daughter?

Have your ever told your parents, "That's not fair!"? How do you think God would respond to your statement (no matter the circumstances) in view of how He commands you to treat your parents?

I grew up as an only child, but always dreamed of having a large family. When I was a teenager, I knew already that I wanted six children. I wanted that sense of brotherhood and sisterhood, to witness what it was like among brothers and sisters, and to be part of a large family. As I thought about my family, I also thought about expectations that I would have from my children versus expectations that were placed on me. One thing that helped me control myself and to make better choices was thinking about my own children. When I had to make a decision that could have consequences, I asked myself: "As a parent, would I want my child doing this?" Sometimes they were activities that I really wanted to do, such as go to a party with my friends where I knew they were drinking or go to other places that my friends were going that I knew were not safe physically or spiritually. However, realizing that my choices may have an influence on my future children really helped me see things from my parents' perspective, which helped me make much better choices, which, in turn, reflected positively on my own parents.

The answer to dealing with parents is respect and earning mutual respect. When you respect your parent's wishes and rules, they will come to mutually respect you, which in turn will also be beneficial to you in the long run. (We'll talk more about that!) Another aspect of your relationship with your parents is respect. Respecting your parents means obedience, respect in the way you talk to them, how you treat them, being honest and truthful to them, and treating them with love, kindness, and value. When you respect your parents, you are fulfilling God's wishes for you. You will have a much better relationship with your parents, which will benefit you in the long run. When you have a mutual relationship with parents, meaning you respect them and display obedience, it is then that you may also start to receive more freedoms, more responsibility, and in the end, more of what *you* want. Even though it is cliché, the truth is that your parents have also had the exact same experiences you are encountering. They know the temptations; they know the good and the bad consequences that can come from many different situations. It is possible that they made poor choices when they were your age, and they just want so much more for you, or they have seen the results the poor choices of their friends, and they want you to have the opportunity to avoid those at all costs. Either way, the most important thing to remember is that your parents love you.

Setting Goals

Think about your parents, your relationship with them, the responsibility commanded of your parents directly from God, and the commands God give you directly as a daughter. As you do, write down three goals dealing with your interactions with your parents. How can you treat them with more respect? How should you treat them? Are there any bad habits you need to break concerning how you interact with your parents? How can you honor your parents and bring honor to your parents?

Goal 1 _____

_____

Goal 2 _____

_____

Goal 3 _____

_____

Remember the meaning of true love: doing what is in your best interest. The next time you get into an argument with your parents, or get angry with them, or feel like they are not being fair, ask yourself these questions:

- Is what I want good for me?

- Will I be safe (spiritually and/or physically)?

- Would I want my own child to be doing what I am asking my parents to let me do?

- Will I bring glory to God doing that activity?

If your answers are all *yes*, then it is probable that your parents are not going to hinder you from going or doing whatever it is that you want to do, but if any of your answers are negative, then it is probable that it is best for you to listen and obey your parents' wisdom. Obedience and treating parents with respect is a trait of a Living Christian.

~Note for those with non-Christian, abusive, strict, or negligent parents~

It is important to know that not all parents are ideal, perfect parents. In fact, most are not, but I do realize that some of you deal with parents who are less than good examples or are possibly neglectful or abusive. In this case your maturity and responsibility for yourself are much higher and important. There is no perfect answer for how to deal with every situation because all circumstances are unique. However, one thing that no child/teenager should have to deal with is abuse. If you are in an abusive situation (verbal, physical, or sexual) you need to get out now. If this is the case, talk to your youth group leader, minister, or a member of your church family that you trust to help you get out of the situation and get you to a safe environment. (You could even talk to a teacher, school counselor, or principal.) The sooner you get out, you can also break the cycle.

A TYPICAL DAY IN THE LIFE OF A HIGH SCHOOL GIRL: LIVING, NOT JUST LIVING

It's Tuesday. Your alarm clock rings at 6:45am. In a haze, blurry visions of sheets, a slowly rotating ceiling fan, arm and hand in a slow swinging motion toward the yellow blinking numbers. It's time to get up. You open one eye slightly to see a faint hint of sunlight shining through the window. You have a faint memory of yesterday, and your brain starts going through the "To Do" list for the day: the big test in world history, band practice in the morning, volleyball practice after school, reading due for English, homework paper due for Spanish, and a couple of equations left to do for algebra. After a quick shower, you brush your teeth, get dressed, fix your hair, and apply your makeup. Voila! You're ready for the day and are out the door.

High school is extremely demanding for any teenager. Stir in the mix of school demands: emotions, hormones, relationships, friends, and home life, and you've got a typical high school girl. With such commitments, where do you find time to do everything you are called to do as a Living Christian? The point of being a Living Christian is just that—living. So far you have studied different ways to be a Living Christian. Each of the topics you've studied thus far is relevant and real to almost every high school girl.

So here is the kicker: How do you integrate live action in all of these different aspects of your life without distraction? How do Living and living coincide? How do you Live and not get distracted by life?

Perspective: What are some responsibilities, obligations, and activities that sometimes (or perhaps frequently) make you lose focus of your true purpose?

The main point here is that sometimes life drags us down and distracts us. Anything that pulls us away from our true purpose can be a distraction. Although those things—whether they are people, activities, or responsibilities—may not be bad or evil, they just need to be put into perspective. The key here is not only organization, but also *prioritization*. Prioritization simply means putting first in our lives what is most important. After thinking about our ministry, we all know that means God, His place, and purpose for our lives. Being a Living Christian is not just about Christian living. It is a state of being, a lifestyle—an all-encompassing state of existence. This doesn't mean that we have to give up everything; it simply means that we must find ways to make Him the priority of our lives. So . . . how do we do it? Depending on your individual situation, that might mean missing a Wednesday evening softball practice to attend Bible class. That might mean not going out on a Saturday night so that you will be fresh and ready for Bible class and worship service on Sunday morning. It might mean not hanging out with specific people anymore because they are a poor influence on you or tempt you to participate in activities you know are wrong or illegal, or you might be present while others are involved in such activity. It might mean breaking up with a current boyfriend who is not a Christian and is not going to help you in your purpose. It might mean quitting the cheerleading squad or dance team because the skirts are too short, the costumes are too revealing or tight, and the dance moves are too provocative. Everything I mentioned here is a negative action, which means you should take yourself out of the situation to avoid any contact with sin or to avoid sinning.

However, prioritization *could* mean your being more proactive in living out your purpose in ways that are more subtle. This could mean asking the coach to change practices from Wednesday night to another night or perhaps an earlier time so that you could still attend practice but not miss out on Bible class (this could be an opportunity to invite some teammates to Bible class!). This could mean your going out Saturday afternoon instead of night, so that you still get to go out, but will also be ready for worship and class on Sunday morning. It could mean your encouraging a group of friends to participate in youth group activities that are uplifting, fun, and in an environment that will bring glory to God. It could mean you also taking your boyfriend to church and youth group activities to help him learn about God, God's will for his life, and by helping him learn about salvation. It could also mean requesting longer skirts, skorts, or even wearing shorts under a cheer-leading skirt, or even helping select costumes that are more modest yet are still cute and fun.

Read James 1:22

"Do not merely _____ of the word,

and so _____ yourselves. Do what it says."

What does this mean?

Read Mark 3:35

Jesus said that when we do God's will we are His _____

and _____ .

Read Luke 6:43-45

Who does the "tree" represent in this verse? What is the meaning of "fruit"?

Read 1 John 2:3-6

This scripture states that we know God if we _____

His _____.

If we do not keep His commandments, we are _____.

What does "abide in Him" mean?

Read 1 John 2:15-17

Do not love the _____ . What does this mean in terms of being a Living Christian?

Verse 17 states that: "the world and its desires pass away . . . but whoever does the will of God lives forever."

What does this verse mean to you?

Through His inspired Word, God calls us to be *doers* of His will. Think about a puzzle. One of my daughter's favorite pastimes is putting together puzzles. She was completing 100-piece puzzles at the age of three, and to this day, she loves putting together new puzzles. When she was first learning how to complete puzzles, she would put together any two pieces at random, finally coming to the point where the puzzle would come together. I taught her how to put together the border first, and then put in the filling pieces. Without the border, the puzzle has no shape, nothing to look to for clues of how to put the rest of the puzzle together. You can put together a puzzle without the border, but it is so much easier when the border is in place. Now think of your life as one big puzzle. The pieces will fit together, they have to, and they will come together whether or not you purposefully put them together, but it is so much easier with the frame already in place: that border to guide you to where the pieces should go. Christ is that border. The example He left for us to follow is solid, unwavering, and clear on what to do and how to do it. If we let Him lay the border for us, the rest of the pieces will fall in place, making our purpose of living as a Living Christian a natural part of our being.

Setting Goals

You have so many options for how you go about living the lifestyle of a Living Christian. When you set goals this time, think of more ways to integrate your lifestyle into all aspects of your life; whether it's at school, at home, with friends, with your boyfriend, etc. How can you intertwine these different aspects of your life to make each piece fit into the puzzle according to the way God calls us to live?

Goal 1 _____

_____

Goal 2 _____

_____

Goal 3 _____

_____

I saw a TV program in which a girl was perceived as strange because she didn't follow any of the popular groups or do what all of the kids were doing. I love this quote from her character: "You laugh at me because I am different, but I laugh at you because you are all the same." How many girls try so hard to be what they think everyone else wants them to be? They are not themselves because they fear that no one will like them or accept them for who they are. How sad is that? And even more sadly, there are myriads of girls like that, just like the quote: They are all the same. But we are called to be different. Although life may seem daunting sometimes and there are many activities and people that may pull you away from being a Living Christian, you must stand firm in your faith and in your convictions. Life is fleeting, which means that it passes by so quickly. It's here and gone. You can enjoy all of God's blessings and do so much in your lifetime when you hold on to Him. There will be tough times, times when you think you cannot pull through, times when you will feel like you are alone, or times when you will mess up. You may be criticized or even left out when you stand up for what you believe in because many times doing the right thing is not easy. Refocusing on God's expectations of you and your life will keep you on the straight and narrow path. There is a part of a poem written by Robert Frost about two paths. The person in the story comes to a split in the road and is faced with two choices. The speaker then says "and I, I took the one less traveled," meaning that that person was unique, individual, and experienced so much more in his lifetime than most people dare to try. When you take that path less traveled, you will have the opportunity to experience so many more of God's blessings and presence in your life than those who take the other paths. Keeping God's commandments, walking as Christ walked, and integrating our Christian walk into our daily lives are traits of a Living Christian.

LEAVING THE YOUTH GROUP–
SPIRITUAL GROWTH

Continual spiritual growth is one of the foundations of being a Living Christian. As a teenager you have more opportunities to be involved in youth and spiritually focused activities throughout the year than people in any other age group. This may include monthly devotionals, Summer Youth Series, youth conferences, youth retreats, summer camp, and other activities set up by youth ministers and others involved in youth ministry. As a teenager, becoming spiritually independent will be the key to continuing your spiritual growth once you leave a youth group. So many people who have not learned spiritual independence end up having difficulties in their spiritual life once they leave home. You don't want to become a person whose faith and lifestyle is based on what your parents believe or "make" you do while you are at home, nor do you want to be dependent on a youth group or youth minister to plan events for you in order to keep you motivated and excited about being a Christian and an active part of the church. Even if you are a younger teenager, you need to know about and be prepared for life beyond high school and living at home. A type of culture shock, when things are just so different than what you are accustomed to, can take place if you are not prepared and ready for life beyond the youth group.

Perspective: What are some activities you are involved in now as part of your youth group that you will not have planned for you as a young adult?

So how do you grow spiritually after you leave the youth group? How do you continue in your spiritual walk? What are some activities in which you can participate now that will help you prepare yourself and learn how to continue to grow spiritually when you are older and more independent?

Here are some simple activities you can do by yourself to keep yourself spiritually active. These are not new ideas. In fact, in almost every book you read about spiritual growth or every sermon or devotional talk you hear you will hear these ideas fleshed out. Everyone concerned with spiritual growth teaches these because not only are they practical, they arc also biblical.

Get Involved in a Small Group

Read Acts 2:40-47

Verse 46 states that the believers "Every day they continued to meet together in the temple courts. They broke bread in their homes." This was one of the first churches mentioned in the Bible. Think about what the text says: They were together every day. They ate together and were at each other's house every day. If you are social, it is probable that you spend a lot of time with your friends, either at their house or yours, during school, and by hanging out and doing things together. When I was a teenager, I had a group of girls with whom I hung out, and we did everything together. We were together during school, lunch, band, and volleyball. We rode to and from school together and usually hung out after school, spending the night at each other's houses, and planning weekend activities. I even worked with one of my friends in an after-school job. This was what the church was like during the ministry of Peter at this time. They hung out together, they ate dinner together, and they were together almost all the time. This wasn't just because they were having fun; it was because by being together, they were able to help one another, to give and receive daily encouragement, and to minister together to one another. They were supported and encouraged every day. By being together, they were stronger in one accord. They were stronger in faith and in ministry. When you are involved in a small group, you can receive this type of encouragement and support one another. Your involvement doesn't have to be daily to still reap the benefits of being with a group of believers to support and encourage each other. Some small groups also do ministry and hold weekly Bible studies. This is the type of support you will need to keep you in touch with others once you leave home. This also will help you create friendships within the church to help you as you venture on your own and learn to stand on your own two feet spiritually. Take the time to invest in a small group.

Read Your Bible

Work on spiritual growth. Knowing your Bible is not passé or just for fun. Knowing your Bible is extremely important and to know Scripture is even biblical. First Peter 3:15 instructs, "But in your hearts revere Christ as Lord. Always be prepared to give an answer to everyone who asks you to give the reason for the hope that you have. But do this with gentleness and respect." In other words, have an answer, be ready to defend your faith with facts and truth, and know your Bible because it helps you to form that defense.

The Bible is also a way for God to speak directly to you, to learn about how you should live, and how you should treat others. In other words, it is a guide for living. Second Timothy 3:16 declares, "All Scripture is God-breathed, and is useful for teaching, rebuking, correcting, and training in righteousness." God gave us Scripture—His Word—so that we can learn about Him, know what plans he has for us (Jeremiah 29:11), to find encouragement and strength in Him, to believe in the hope He gives us, and for so many thousands of other reasons all so that He can reach us and help us. And to know all of this, you must know your Bible so that you have the information to share with others and to teach and instruct others. Never stop reading your Bible. Never stop learning about the hope and salvation that lies in God and His promises to us.

Be Active in Ministry

Even after you leave the youth group, there are still many ways to be involved in ministry. Ministry can include teaching children's Bible classes, helping out in the food pantry, visiting the sick, visiting the shut-ins, or simply helping where you are needed. Depending on the congregation you attend, the opportunities for ministry are limitless, whether it is ministry supported by the church or a ministry you create. Ministry is serving others, helping, being a servant of God. When you help and serve, you are putting others before yourself and fulfilling a need, however I have always found that when I go to help and serve others, my cup always gets filled in the process. Ministry helps keep you faithful and involved, and it also helps you fortify relationships within the church. When you minister together you can't help but grow together. Being active in ministry is important for spiritual growth as it keeps you in-sync with your purpose. Ministry should be on purpose as part of being a Living Christian.

Do not Forsake the Assembly

Just like being part of a small group is important, it is just as important to be part of the whole assembly. The purpose of the assembly is to glorify God. You come together with other believers of all ages to worship and glorify God and to partake in the Lord's Supper—a weekly reminder of what Jesus did for us and a time to refocus for the week. Every assembly is important as an opportunity to give and receive encouragement. When you attend, you also have accountability from other members. There are deacons and elders to whom you can talk if you need extra encouragement or support. You also have church members on whom you can depend for help or support when you need it, and you also offer yourself as support and help for those who might need it from you at any time.

Going to church may also open up ministry opportunities such as teaching a Bible class or helping with the VBS ministry or help you find a small group. Simply put, being part of the assembly also helps you start your week off the way that God intended—by worshiping Him in joint union with His church.

All of these activities are important for spiritual growth and spiritual maintenance. Through this study, we have focused on many different ways to fall into temptation and to fall away from God and His purpose for our lives. And falling is so easy to do. Matthew wrote "narrow is the road" (Matthew 7:14), meaning that not many people will follow this path in its entirety. At times, it will be difficult, but for those who do, and who remain faithful (not perfect, but faithful), the rewards will be great, more awesome than we can even imagine. "Now to Him who is able to do immeasurably more than all we ask or imagine, to him be glory" (Ephesians 3:20). Matthew 10:22 declares: "But the one who stands firm to the end will be saved." To those who follow the wide path that "leads to destruction," which is easy, they will have their reward, which is seeking their selfish desires.

Setting Goals

We have to stay firm, steady, consistent, and faithful in our walk with God, always keeping in mind the hope that we have through Him. Maintaining spiritual growth is just that—maintenance. Just as we all hear every day about how we need to maintain our health by eating right, exercising, and taking care of ourselves, what we do to maintain spiritually is just as important, if not much more important. Set some goals for yourself. Make a plan for how you will maintain spiritual growth after you leave home.

Goal 1 _____

_____

Goal 2 _____

_____

Goal 3 _____

_____

Exercise, exercise, exercise! Your spiritual health, that is. As discussed previously, don't let anything get in the way of your living out your purpose, and to do that even more effectively, you need the power of God behind you: the knowledge of His Word, the power of the wisdom that comes from the Bible, and the power of support and encouragement that comes from your church family. Spiritual growth is a characteristic of a Living Christian.

LIVING OUT YOUR PURPOSE: THE GREAT COMMISSION

In the months following Jesus' return to earth after His amazing and miraculous resurrection, He appeared to many people in different areas. He encouraged the disciples and the apostles by appearing to them and showing them that He had overpowered death and affirming their faith in Him by letting them see the holes in his hands and his pierced side. At the end of His time on earth, He left one powerful set of instructions for us to follow and put them in the most direct and simple manner to understand.

"Therefore go and make disciples of all nations, baptizing them in the name of the Father and of the Son and of the Holy Spirit, and teaching them to obey everything I have commanded you. And surely, I am with you always, to the very end of the age" (Matthew 28:19-20).

Perspective: This is a personal commandment to all of us. How do you feel God is leading you to "go into all the world"?

This one command, this direct and simple instruction sums up exactly what we are to do with our lives and how to live out our purpose. And even so much more powerful is that this commandment is given to you and to me. We started this study in Chapter 1 learning about this purpose: to share the message of Christ with others. As we have discussed within this study, this is your purpose, your goal, and priority in all areas of your life. The power of the last commandment of Christ, the empowerment that it gives us is still so amazing and inspiring. At the beginning of this study, you wrote down three goals dealing with living your purpose and following the example of Christ. I want you to take a few minutes to reflect on what you wrote, and think about your goals. Write a brief response to the following questions:

How have you been working on them?

How has this changed your lifestyle or has it?

How has this impacted you or has it impacted you in any way?

Do your goals need to be revised?

Setting Goals

Keep in mind that Jesus was speaking directly to you and to me, and to all believers and His followers when He charged us with spreading the gospel. Sometimes it's hard for us to think of Jesus in terms of speaking directly to us when we read His words in the Bible. At this point in the story of Jesus' time on earth, He had been resurrected for some time and was about to leave, to ascend into the heavens. Pretend that He is standing next to you at this moment, repeating those exact words directly to you. Do you feel more adamant or passionate about following through with His direct orders? Do you believe that all of those people standing there listening to Him speak felt more passion or excitement about this last command? Thinking about the Great Commission, write three goals specifically dealing with when/where/how you are going to continue or start following the Great Commission.

Goal 1 _____

_____

Goal 2 _____

_____

Goal 3 _____

_____

I recently saw a movie about a teenage boy who went through a tragic experience. Through this experience, he met a minister who encouraged him, helped him, and ultimately, led him to Christ. There was a moment in the movie where he was sitting with other teens and the youth minister was giving a sermon, but none of the teens were listening or reacting. The boy got so upset that he stood up and yelled at them, "What's the point of all of this if you don't let it change you?" I pose this same question to you:

What's the point of all of this if you don't let it change you?

I sincerely hope that you have taken this study to heart and that it not only has changed you but has inspired you. I hope that this has encouraged you to take a serious look at your life and how you are living it and that you have changed what you needed to change. Maybe you were already on the straight and narrow and this has encouraged you and given the confirmation and affirmation you needed to continue living as a Living Christian. Maybe you were faking, just going through the motions, and this helped push you into really doing it. Maybe you just didn't get it, or never knew it, and you have completely turned your life around. Whatever your situation is, I hope that you have learned and have grown, and that you will continue to learn and grow. Be a Living Christian—live in Christ so that He may live through you! To conclude, I share this prayer from Hebrews 13:18-21.

"Pray for us. We are sure that we have a clear conscience and desire to live honorably in every way. I particularly urge you to pray so that I may be restored to you soon. Now may the God of peace, who through the blood of the eternal covenant brought back from the dead our Lord Jesus, that great Shepherd of the sheep, equip you with everything good for doing his will, and may he work in us what is pleasing to him, through Jesus Christ, to whom be glory for ever and ever. Amen."

CPSIA information can be obtained at www.ICGtesting.com
Printed in the USA
LVOW01s0505180415

435000LV00004B/7/P

9 780890 986981